Duffy

by Iain Gray

D1465347

Lang**Syne**

PUBLISHING

WRITING *to* REMEMBER

LangSyne
PUBLISHING
WRITING *to* REMEMBER

E-mail: info@lang-syne.co.uk

Distributed in the Republic of Ireland by Portfolio Group,
Kilbarrack Ind. Est. Kilbarrack, Dublin 5.
T:00353(01) 839 4918 F:00353(01) 839 5826
sales@portfoliogroup.ie
www.portfoliogroup.ie

Design by Dorothy Meikle   Printed by Ricoh Print Scotland

ISBN 978-1-85217-251-0

Duffy

MOTTO:
By virtue and deeds.

CREST:
An angel.

NAME variations include:
Ó Dubthaigh *(Gaelic)*
O' Duffy
Dowey
Duffie
Duffey
Doohey

Chapter one:
Origins of Irish surnames

**According to an old saying, there are two types of Irish –
those who actually are Irish and those who wish they were.**

This sentiment is only one example of the allure that the
high romance and drama of the proud nation's history holds
for thousands of people scattered across the world today.

It's a sad fact, however, that the vast majority of Irish
surnames are found far beyond Irish shores, rather than on
the Emerald Isle itself.

The population stood at around eight million souls in
1841, but today it stands at fewer than six million.

This is mainly a tragic consequence of the potato
famine, also known as the Great Hunger, which devastated
Ireland between 1845 and 1849.

The Irish peasantry had become almost wholly reliant
for basic sustenance on the potato, first introduced from the
Americas in the seventeenth century.

When the crop was hit by a blight, at least 800,000
people starved to death while an estimated two million
others were forced to seek a new life far from their native
shores – particularly in America, Canada, and Australia.

The effects of the potato blight continued until about
1851, by which time a firm pattern of emigration had
become established.

Ireland's loss, however, was to the gain of the countries in which the immigrants settled, contributing enormously, as their descendants do today, to the well being of the nations in which their forefathers settled.

But those who were forced through dire circumstance to establish a new life in foreign parts never forgot their roots, or the proud heritage and traditions of the land that gave them birth.

Nor do their descendants.

It is a heritage that is inextricably bound up in the colourful variety of Irish names themselves – and the origin and history of these names forms an integral part of the vibrant drama that is the nation's history, one of both glorious fortune and tragic misfortune.

This history is well documented, and one of the most important and fascinating of the earliest sources are *The Annals of the Four Masters*, compiled between 1632 and 1636 by four friars at the Franciscan Monastery in County Donegal.

Compiled from earlier sources, and purporting to go back to the Biblical Deluge, much of the material takes in the mythological origins and history of Ireland and the Irish.

This includes tales of successive waves of invaders and settlers such as the Fomorians, the Partholonians, the Nemedians, the Fir Bolgs, the Tuatha De Danann, and the Laigain.

Of particular interest are the *Milesian Genealogies*,

because the majority of Irish clans today claim a descent from either Heremon, Ir, or Heber – three of the sons of Milesius, a king of what is now modern day Spain.

These sons invaded Ireland in the second millennium B.C, apparently in fulfilment of a mysterious prophecy received by their father.

This Milesian lineage is said to have ruled Ireland for nearly 3,000 years, until the island came under the sway of England's King Henry II in 1171 following what is known as the Cambro-Norman invasion.

This is an important date not only in Irish history in general, but for the effect the invasion subsequently had for Irish surnames.

'Cambro' comes from the Welsh, and 'Cambro-Norman' describes those Welsh knights of Norman origin who invaded Ireland.

But they were invaders who stayed, inter-marrying with the native Irish population and founding their own proud dynasties that bore Cambro-Norman names such as Archer, Barbour, Brannagh, Fitzgerald, Fitzgibbon, Fleming, Joyce, Plunkett, and Walsh – to name only a few.

These 'Cambro-Norman' surnames that still flourish throughout the world today form one of the three main categories in which Irish names can be placed – those of Gaelic-Irish, Cambro-Norman, and Anglo-Irish.

Previous to the Cambro-Norman invasion of the twelfth century, and throughout the earlier invasions and settlement of those wild bands of sea rovers known as the Vikings in the eighth and ninth centuries, the population of the island was relatively small, and it was normal for a person to be identified through the use of only a forename.

But as population gradually increased and there were many more people with the same forename, surnames were adopted to distinguish one person, or one community, from another.

Individuals identified themselves with their own particular tribe, or 'tuath', and this tribe – that also became known as a clann, or clan – took its name from some distinguished ancestor who had founded the clan.

The Gaelic-Irish form of the name Kelly, for example, is Ó Ceallaigh, or O'Kelly, indicating descent from an original 'Ceallaigh', with the 'O' denoting 'grandson of.' The name was later anglicised to Kelly.

The prefix 'Mac' or 'Mc', meanwhile, as with the clans of the Scottish Highlands, denotes 'son of.'

Although the Irish clans had much in common with their Scottish counterparts, one important difference lies in what are known as 'septs', or branches, of the clan.

Septs of Scottish clans were groups who often bore an entirely different name from the clan name but were under the clan's protection.

In Ireland, septs were groups that shared the same name and who could be found scattered throughout the four provinces of Ulster, Leinster, Munster, and Connacht.

The 'golden age' of the Gaelic-Irish clans, infused as their veins were with the blood of Celts, pre-dates the Viking invasions of the eighth and ninth centuries and the Norman invasion of the twelfth century, and the sacred heart of the country was the Hill of Tara, near the River Boyne, in County Meath.

Known in Gaelic as 'Teamhar na Rí', or Hill of Kings, it was the royal seat of the 'Ard Rí Éireann', or High King of Ireland, to whom the petty kings, or chieftains, from the island's provinces were ultimately subordinate.

It was on the Hill of Tara, beside a stone pillar known as the Irish 'Lia Fáil', or Stone of Destiny, that the High Kings were inaugurated and, according to legend, this stone would emit a piercing screech that could be heard all over Ireland when touched by the hand of the rightful king.

The Hill of Tara is today one of the island's main tourist attractions.

Opposition to English rule over Ireland, established in the wake of the Cambro-Norman invasion, broke out frequently and the harsh solution adopted by the powerful forces of the Crown was to forcibly evict the native Irish from their lands.

These lands were then granted to Protestant colonists, or 'planters', from Britain.

Many of these colonists, ironically, came from Scotland and were the descendants of the original 'Scotti', or 'Scots', who gave their name to Scotland after migrating there in the fifth century A.D., from the north of Ireland.

Colonisation entailed harsh penal laws being imposed on the majority of the native Irish population, stripping them practically of all of their rights.

The Crown's main bastion in Ireland was Dublin and its environs, known as the Pale, and it was the dispossessed peasantry who lived outside this Pale, desperately striving to eke out a meagre living.

It was this that gave rise to the modern-day expression of someone or something being 'beyond the pale'.

Attempts were made to stamp out all aspects of the ancient Gaelic-Irish culture, to the extent that even to bear a Gaelic-Irish name was to invite discrimination.

This is why many Gaelic-Irish names were anglicised with, for example, and noted above, Ó Ceallaigh, or O'Kelly, being anglicised to Kelly.

Succeeding centuries have seen strong revivals of Gaelic-Irish consciousness, however, and this has led to many families reverting back to the original form of their name, while the language itself is frequently found on the fluent tongues of an estimated 90,000 to 145,000 of the island's population.

Ireland's turbulent history of religious and political strife is one that lasted well into the twentieth century, a landmark century that saw the partition of the island into the twenty-six counties of the independent Republic of

Ireland, or Eire, and the six counties of Northern Ireland, or Ulster.

Dublin, originally founded by Vikings, is now a vibrant and truly cosmopolitan city while the proud city of Belfast is one of the jewels in the crown of Ulster.

It was Saint Patrick who first brought the light of Christianity to Ireland in the fifth century A.D.

Interpretations of this Christian message have varied over the centuries, often leading to bitter sectarian conflict – but the many intricately sculpted Celtic Crosses found all over the island are symbolic of a unity that crosses the sectarian divide.

It is an image that fuses the 'old gods' of the Celts with Christianity.

All the signs from the early years of this new millennium indicate that sectarian strife may soon become a thing of the past – with the Irish and their many kinsfolk across the world, be they Protestant or Catholic, finding common purpose in the rich tapestry of their shared heritage.

Chapter two:
Celtic twilight

The ancestors of bearers of what has now become the proud name of Duffy were originally to be found all over the Emerald Isle from earliest times, existing as distinct family groupings in their own right.

In its Gaelic form of Ó Dubthaigh the name stems from the personal name 'Dubthach', indicating 'dark one' and probably a reference to someone with dark, or black, hair – while other sources assert the derivation is from 'of the dark house.'

Originally found in present day Irish counties that included Dublin, Kildare, and Meath, the ancestors of the Duffys of today also spread to other present day counties that include those of Donegal, Roscommon, Louth, and Monaghan.

Their heritage is truly illustrious, particularly that of the Monaghan sept from the ancient province of Ulster and their related family branches.

This is a rich and colourful heritage that can be traced back to no less than Conall Gulban, a son of the great warrior king Niall Noíghiallach, better known to posterity as Niall of the Nine Hostages.

The dramatic life and times of this ancestor of the Duffys and a number of other proud Irish clans are steeped in stirring Celtic myth and legend.

The youngest son of Eochaidh Mugmedon, king of the province of Connacht, his mother died in childbirth and he was brought up by his evil stepmother Mongfhinn who, for reasons best known to herself, was determined that he should die.

She accordingly abandoned him naked on the Hill of Tara, inauguration site of the Ard Rí, or High Kings, of Ireland, but he was found by a wandering bard who took him back to his father.

One legend is that Mongfhinn sent Niall and his four brothers – Brian, Fiachra, Ailill, and Fergus – to a renowned prophet who was also a blacksmith to determine which of them would succeed their father as Ard Rí.

The blacksmith, known as Sitchin, set the lads a task by deliberately setting fire to his forge.

Niall's brothers ran in and came out carrying the spearheads, fuel, hammers, and barrels of beer that they had rescued, but Niall staggered out clutching the heavy anvil so vital to the blacksmith's trade.

By this deed, Sitchin prophesied that Niall would be the one who would take on the glorious mantle of kingship.

Another prophetic incident occurred one day while Niall and his brothers were engaged in the hunt.

Thirsty from their efforts they encountered an ugly old woman who offered them water – but only in return for a kiss.

Three of the lads, no doubt repelled by her green teeth

and scaly skin, refused. Fiachra pecked her lightly on the cheek and, by this act, she prophesied that he would one day reign at Tara – but only briefly.

The bold Niall, however, kissed her fully on the lips. The hag then demanded that he should now have full sexual intercourse with her and, undaunted, he did so.

Through this action she was suddenly transformed into a stunningly beautiful young woman known as Flaithius, or Royalty, who predicted that he would become the greatest High King of Ireland.

His stepmother Mongfhinn later tried to poison him, but accidentally took the deadly potion herself and died.

This legend relates to what was known as the Festival of Mongfhinn, or Feis na Samhan (the Fest of Samhain), because it was on the evening of October 31, on Samhain's Eve, that the poisoning incident is said to have taken place.

It was believed for centuries in Ireland that, on Samhain Eve, Mongfhinn's warped and wicked spirit would roam the land in hungry search of children's souls.

The Festival, or Feast, of Samhain, is better known today as Halloween.

Niall became Ard Rí in 379 A.D. and embarked on the series of military campaigns and other daring adventures that would subsequently earn him the title of Niall of the Nine Hostages.

The nine countries and territories into which he raided and took hostages for ransom were the Irish provinces of

Munster, Leinster, Connacht, and Ulster, Britain, and the territories of the Saxons, Morini, Picts, and Dalriads.

Niall's most famous hostage was a young lad known as Succat, son of Calpernius, a Romano-Briton who lived in the area of present day Milford Haven, on the Welsh coast.

Later known as Patricius, or Patrick, he became renowned as Ireland's patron saint, St. Patrick, responsible for bringing the light of Christianity to the island in the early years of the fifth century A.D.

Raiding in Gaul, in the area of Boulogne-sur-mer in present day France, Niall was ambushed and killed by one of his treacherous subjects in 405 A.D.

But his legacy survived through the royal dynasties and clans founded by his sons – not least Conall Gulban, who laid the foundations of the Duffy septs to be found in the northern reaches of the island.

It is perhaps rather ironic, bearing in mind that the Duffys can trace a descent from Niall of the Nine Hostages who kidnapped the future St. Patrick, that they can also trace a descent from not only Dubthach, patron saint of what is now the diocese of Raphoe, in Co. Donegal, but also St. Bridget, one of Ireland's national patron saints.

It was in the present day parish of Lower Templecrone that Dubthach carried out his missionary work, establishing a religious community at Termon. His feast day is celebrated on February 5.

Along with St. Patrick and St Colmcille, St. Bridget is

one of Ireland's three revered patron saints – and Duffys of today can be justly proud of the fact that they share a kinship with her.

Known today as 'Mary of the Gaels', she is believed to have been born in Fochart in about 450 A.D and to have died in 523 A.D.

Of particular interest to the Duffys is that from an early period she was known as 'Bridget, the daughter of Dubthach of Cill Dara' meaning 'Bridget Duffy of Kildare.'

Also known as 'Brigit', she was the daughter of a slave-woman through her mother's relationship with a 'Dubthach' (Duffy) chieftain.

Jealous of her husband's relationship with the woman the chieftain's wife ordered that she should be sent from their household, along with her daughter, and sold to a Druid.

Although Druids were members of the elite Celtic caste that regulated the worship of what Christianity termed the pagan gods, it appears that Bridget was baptised into the Christian faith and later returned to her father's home – by this time an exceedingly beautiful young woman.

Many men offered her their hand in marriage, but Bridget was more concerned in helping the poor – often at the expense of her father, whose goods she gave away in charitable acts.

This, combined with the fact that she had aroused the jealousy of the chief's wife, led to the decision being taken that she be sold to a king who ruled in the north of the province of Leinster.

While her father entered the king's stronghold to barter with the king for his daughter, a beggar approached Bridget. Having no gold or other wealth to give him, she gave him her father's magnificent sword.

While her father was understandably angry the Leinster king was impressed by her action, stating 'her merit is higher before God than before men.'

He then presented her father with an even more magnificent sword and set Bridget free.

According to tradition she then became a nun and, returning to Kildare, established a church.

Along with St. Patrick and St. Colmcille, the remains of St. Bridget were later interred in a triple vault at Downpatrick.

Discovered in 1185, they were re-interred in Downpatrick Cathedral but their monuments were destroyed during the religious reformation of Henry VIII in the early sixteenth century.

The head of St. Bridget was later recovered and is now a treasured relic in a Jesuit Church in Lisbon, in Portugal.

In its attempt to eradicate worship of the old pagan gods and goddesses, early Christianity 'hijacked' many of the pagan elements and incorporated them into its own customs and practices under a Christian veneer.

Many churches, for example, were built on the site of

ancient places held dear by those who had worshipped the old gods.

No less so than with the Celtic goddess of healing, Bridget, or Brigit: her annual festival was held February 1 – and this was taken over as the feast day of St. Bridget.

Still in the twilit realms of ancient Celtic belief the Duffys of today are also a sept of the proud Scottish clan of Macfie, whose territory for centuries was the west coast Inner Hebridean island of Colonsay.

Along with the Macfies the Duffys are believed to be endowed with mystic powers.

This relates to a strange legend of how a Macfie had captured a Selkie, or seal woman, who had cast off her fur and become transformed into a beautiful woman.

The Macfie married her and hid her fur so that she could never leave him by returning to the sea and, in true fairy tale fashion, the pair lived happily ever after.

Celtic myth and legend apart, the Duffys embraced the Christian faith with a passion, producing many distinguished ecclesiastics.

John A. Duffy, born in 1884 and who died in 1944, was the 7th Bishop of Buffalo, New York, while Joseph Duffy, born in 1934 in Newbliss, Co. Monaghan is, at the time of writing, Roman Catholic Bishop of Clogher, in his native Ireland.

In 1979 he became the first Irish Bishop to be appointed by Pope John Paul II.

Chapter three:
Wars of independence

The ancestors of the Duffys of today, in common with other native Irish clans, were far from immune to the many trials and tribulations to which the island was subjected over the centuries.

One of the most seminal events in Ireland's long history was the late twelfth century Cambro-Norman invasion of the island, followed by the domination of the forces of the English Crown. Affecting the future course of the island's affairs in general and the lives of native Irish such as the Duffys in particular, its importance cannot be overestimated.

Twelfth century Ireland was far from being a unified nation, split up as it was into territories ruled over by squabbling chieftains who ruled as kings in their own right – and this inter-clan rivalry worked to the advantage of the invaders.

In a series of bloody conflicts one chieftain, or king, would occasionally gain the upper hand over his rivals, and by 1156 the most powerful was Muirchertach MacLochlainn, king of the powerful O'Neills.

The equally powerful Rory O'Connor, king of the province of Connacht, opposed him but he increased his power and influence by allying himself with Dermot MacMurrough, king of Leinster.

MacLochlainn and MacMurrough were aware that the main key to the kingdom of Ireland was the thriving trading port of Dublin that had been established by invading Vikings, or Ostmen, in 852 A.D.

Dublin was taken by the combined forces of the Leinster and Connacht kings, but when MacLochlainn died the Dubliners rose up in revolt and overthrew the unpopular MacMurrough.

A triumphant Rory O'Connor entered Dublin and was later inaugurated as Ard Rí, but MacMurrough refused to accept defeat and appealed for help from England's Henry II in unseating O'Connor.

The English monarch agreed to help MacMurrough, but distanced himself from direct action by delegating his Norman subjects in Wales with the task.

These ambitious and battle-hardened barons and knights had first settled in Wales following the Norman Conquest of England in 1066 and, with an eye on rich booty, plunder, and lands, were only too eager to obey their sovereign's wishes and furnish MacMurrough with aid.

MacMurrough rallied powerful barons such as Robert Fitzstephen and Maurice Fitzgerald to his cause, along with Gilbert de Clare, Earl of Pembroke.

The mighty Norman war machine soon moved into action, and so fierce and disciplined was their onslaught on the forces of Rory O'Connor and his allies that by 1171 they had re-captured Dublin and other strategically important territories.

Henry II now began to take cold feet over the venture, realising that he may have created a rival in the form of a separate Norman kingdom in Ireland and, in October of 1171, he landed on the island with a large army at his back with the aim of curbing the power of his Cambro-Norman barons.

But protracted war between the king and his barons was averted when they submitted to the royal will, promising homage and allegiance in return for holding the territories they had conquered in the king's name.

Henry also received the reluctant submission and homage of many of the Irish chieftains.

English dominion over Ireland was ratified through the Treaty of Windsor of 1175, under the terms of which Rory O'Connor, for example, was allowed to rule territory unoccupied by the Normans in the role of a vassal of the king.

The English grip on the island tightened like a noose, and the understandable result was a series of bloody rebellions over the following centuries.

The cauldron of discontent boiled over in 1641 in the form of a rebellion by the Catholic landowners against the English Crown's policy of settling, or 'planting' loyal Protestants on Irish land.

This policy had started during the reign from 1491 to 1547 of Henry VIII, whose Reformation effectively outlawed the established Roman Catholic faith throughout his dominions.

This settlement of loyal Protestants in Ireland continued throughout the subsequent reigns of Elizabeth I, James I (James VI of Scotland), and Charles I.

In the insurrection that exploded in 1641, at least 2,000 Protestant settlers were massacred at the hands of Catholic landowners and their native Irish peasantry, while thousands more were driven from their lands.

Revenge came in August of 1649 in the form of England's Oliver Cromwell, known as the Lord Protector, who descended on Ireland at the head of a 20,000-strong army that landed at Ringford, near Dublin.

He soon held Ireland in a grip of iron, allowing him to implement what amounted to a policy of ethnic cleansing.

His troopers were given free rein to hunt down and kill priests, while Catholic estates were confiscated.

A series of harsh penal measures against Catholics followed over the succeeding decades, and the result was a rebellion that erupted in 1798 in a bid to restore Irish freedom and independence.

The roots of the 1798 Rising are complex, but in essence it was sparked off by a fusion of sectarian and agrarian unrest and a burning desire for political reform that had been shaped by the French revolutionary slogan of 'liberty, equality, and fraternity.'

A movement had come into existence that embraced

middle-class intellectuals and the oppressed peasantry, and if this loosely bound movement could be said to have had a leader, it was Wolfe Tone, a Protestant from Kildare and leading light of a radical republican movement known as the United Irishmen.

Despite attempts by the British government to concede a degree of agrarian and political reform, it was a case of far too little and much too late, and by 1795 the United Irishmen, through Wolfe Tone, were receiving help from France – Britain's enemy.

A French invasion fleet was despatched to Ireland in December of 1796, but it was scattered by storms off Bantry Bay. Two years later, in the summer of 1798, rebellion broke out on the island.

The first flames of revolt were fanned in Ulster, but soon died out, only to be replaced by a much more serious conflagration centred mainly in Co. Wexford.

Rebel victory was achieved at the battle of Oulart Hill, followed by another victory at the battle of Three Rocks, but the peasant army was no match for the 20,000 troops or so that descended on Wexford.

Defeat followed at the battle of Vinegar Hill on 21 June, followed by another decisive defeat at Kilcumney Hill five days later.

An Act of Union between Great Britain and Ireland was passed in 1880, and this served to fuel the flames of further rebellion.

There was a short-lived and abortive rebellion in the summer of 1848 by a movement known as the Young Irelanders, who sought repeal of the union.

One of its leading lights was Charles Gavan Duffy, born in 1816 in the town of Monaghan, in Co. Monaghan.

Jailed for 'seditious conspiracy' for articles that had appeared under his editorship in the *Young Irelanders'* newspaper, The Nation, he was later released and went on to found a tenants' rights league.

But by 1856, pessimistic over the prospect of Ireland ever gaining independence from Britain, he immigrated with his family to Australia.

It was here that both he and his descendants flourished.

He served as Premier of Victoria from 1871 to 1872, being knighted a year later. He died in 1903.

One of his sons, Charles Gavan Duffy, served as Chief Justice of the High Court of Australia from 1931 to 1935.

Chapter four:
On the world stage

Bearers of the Duffy name have thrived, and continue to thrive, in a truly diverse range of pursuits.

Born in 1949 in Townsend, Montana, **Patrick Duffy** is the American actor of Irish descent best known for his role as Bobby James Ewing in the popular American television soap opera *Dallas* – a role he played between 1978 and 1985 and between 1986 and 1991.

His first major role before *Dallas* was as Mark Harris in the television series *Man from Atlantis*, while roles he has played since the demise of *Dallas* include on the American television sitcom *Step by Step*.

While his many dramatic roles have been based on fiction, one real-life tragedy that hit the popular actor was the murder of his parents, Terrance and Marie Duffy, by two men during the robbery of a bar owned by them in Montana.

Julia Duffy is the American actress who, every year from 1984 to 1990, earned Emmy Award nominations for her role in the *Newhart* television series.

Born in 1951 in Minneapolis, she has appeared in films such as the 1981 *Night Warning* and, from the same year, *Cutter's Way*.

Also on the stage **Karen Duffy** is the actress, television personality and model who was born in 1962 in New York

City, while **Gerald Duffy**, born in 1896 and who died in 1928, was an award-winning American screenwriter of the era of silent film.

Born in Dublin in 1952, **Martin Duffy** is the Irish writer and filmmaker whose many credits include the 1996 *The Boy from Mercury*, the 1999 *The Bumblebee Files*, and the 2000 *The Testimony of Taliesin Jones*.

He is also the author of a number of children's books.

Inducted into the Canadian Association of Broadcasters Hall of Fame in 1994, **Mike Duffy** is the popular television journalist who was born in 1946 in Charlottetown, Prince Edward Island.

At the time of writing he is host of *Mike Duffy Live* and *Countdown with Mike Duffy* and the Ottowa editor for CTV NewsNet.

Born in 1966 in Drogheda, **Jim Duffy** is the Irish political commentator and historian who also makes regular television appearances in his native country.

In the world of publishing **James Duffy**, born in 1809 in Co. Monaghan and who died in 1871, was the major Irish publisher who founded the company of James Duffy and Sons.

Among the many books, magazines, bibles, and missals the company produced were the *Illustrated Dublin Journal* and *Duffy's Irish Catholic Magazine*.

On a musical note **Uriah Duffy**, born in Rhode Island, is the American bass guitarist who, at the time of writing, plays for the rock band Whitesnake and who has also played for artistes that include Christina Aguilera, Carmen Appice, and Pat Travers.

From rock music to classical music **Thomas Duffy**, born in 1955, is the American conductor and composer of classical music who has conducted orchestras and bands throughout the world, while in the world of popular music **Keith Duffy**, born in 1974 in Dublin, is a member of the best-selling band Boyzone.

He also pursues a career as an actor.

Born in 1938 in Ilford, Essex, Brian John Duffy is better known as **Jet Black**, one of the founder members in the mid-1970s of the punk rock/new wave band the Stranglers.

Also in the world of music **Billy Duffy**, born in 1961 in Manchester, is the guitarist with the band the Cult whose best-selling albums include the 1984 *Dreamtime* and the 2007 *Born Into This*.

In the competitive world of sport **Hugh Duffy**, born in 1866 in Cranston, Rhode Island, and who died in 1954, was a leading late nineteenth century and early twentieth century player and manager in Major League Baseball.

Teams he played for included the Chicago Pirates, Boston Reds, and Philadelphia Phillies, while teams he managed included the Milwaukee Brewers, Chicago White Sox, and Boston Red Sox.

He was inducted into the Baseball Hall of Fame in 1945.

In contemporary times **Chris Duffy**, born in 1980 in

Vermont, is the Major League Baseball player who, at the time of writing, plays for the Pittsburgh Pirates.

In the creative world of art Patrick William Duffy, better known as **P.W. Duffy**, is the American artist who was born in 1966 in Houston, Texas.

Best known for his innovative scenic paintings and murals, one of his most celebrated works is a vast 400ft long mural, executed in 1998, of a guitar on the exterior of the Hard Rock Cafe premises in Nashville, Tennessee.

Taking to the skies, **Brian Duffy** is the retired colonel with the United Sates Air Force and former NASA astronaut who was born in 1953 in Boston.

A veteran of more than forty space flights – logging an impressive more than forty days in space – he is, at the time of writing, vice president and associate programme manager for the Lockheed Martin Corporation.

Duffys have also gained distinction on the field of battle – with no less than two Irish bearers of the name recipients of the Victoria Cross, the highest award for gallantry for British and Commonwealth forces.

Born in 1805 in Co. Westmeath **Thomas Duffy** was a private in the 1st Madras Fusiliers during the Indian Mutiny.

He was awarded the Victoria Cross following his part in an action at Lucknow in September of 1857 when, under extremely heavy fire, he helped to retrieve a 24-pounder gun before it fell into the hands of the enemy.

He died in his native Dublin a year later.

Another recipient of the Victoria Cross was **James Duffy**, born in 1889 in Crolly, Co. Donegal.

He was a private and a stretcher-bearer with the 6th Battalion, The Royal Iniskilling Fusiliers when, during a First World War action in Palestine in December of 1917, he managed to rescue badly wounded comrades from the field of battle.

He died in 1969.

Born in 1871 in Cobourg, Ontario, **Francis P. Duffy** later immigrated over the border to the Unites States to settle in New York City, where he was ordained as a priest in 1896.

By the time of the outbreak of the First World War in 1914 Father Duffy had already gained a reputation for himself as a selfless and tireless worker among his parishioners in the Bronx.

But it was as a military chaplain with the 69th New York Regiment, later known as the 165th U.S. Infantry Regiment, but better known as the 'Fighting 69th', that he gained even wider repute.

Serving with the regiment on the battlefields of the Western Front, Father Duffy's contribution to the morale of the regiment was so great that at one time he was seriously considered for the post of regimental commander.

Frequently accompanying stretcher-bearers onto the carnage of the battlefield, his dedication and bravery was recognised with a host of awards and decorations –

including the Distinguished Service Cross, The Conspicuous Service Cross (New York State), the Croix de Guerre, and the French Legion d' Honneur.

Following the end of the conflict he worked as a pastor of Holy Cross Church in the Hell's Kitchen area of New York City, near Times Square.

An area of Times Square known as Duffy Square, and containing a statue of him, was named in his honour.

He died in 1932, while his war experiences were fictionalised in the movie *The Fighting 69th*.

Key dates in Ireland's history from the first settlers to the formation of the Irish Republic:

circa 7000 B.C.	Arrival and settlement of Stone Age people.
circa 3000 B.C.	Arrival of settlers of New Stone Age period.
circa 600 B.C.	First arrival of the Celts.
200 A.D.	Establishment of Hill of Tara, Co. Meath, as seat of the High Kings.
circa 432 A.D.	Christian mission of St. Patrick.
800-920 A.D.	Invasion and subsequent settlement of Vikings.
1002 A.D.	Brian Boru recognised as High King.
1014	Brian Boru killed at battle of Clontarf.
1169-1170	Cambro-Norman invasion of the island.
1171	Henry II claims Ireland for the English Crown.
1366	Statutes of Kilkenny ban marriage between native Irish and English.
1529-1536	England's Henry VIII embarks on religious Reformation.
1536	Earl of Kildare rebels against the Crown.
1541	Henry VIII declared King of Ireland.
1558	Accession to English throne of Elizabeth I.
1565	Battle of Affane.
1569-1573	First Desmond Rebellion.
1579-1583	Second Desmond Rebellion.
1594-1603	Nine Years War.
1606	'Plantation' of Scottish and English settlers.
1607	Flight of the Earls.
1632-1636	Annals of the Four Masters compiled.
1641	Rebellion over policy of plantation and other grievances.
1649	Beginning of Cromwellian conquest.
1688	Flight into exile in France of Catholic Stuart monarch James II as Protestant Prince William of Orange invited to take throne of England along with his wife, Mary.
1689	William and Mary enthroned as joint monarchs; siege of Derry.
1690	Jacobite forces of James defeated by William at battle of the Boyne (July) and Dublin taken.

1691	Athlone taken by William; Jacobite defeats follow at Aughrim, Galway, and Limerick; conflict ends with Treaty of Limerick (October) and Irish officers allowed to leave for France.
1695	Penal laws introduced to restrict rights of Catholics; banishment of Catholic clergy.
1704	Laws introduced constricting rights of Catholics in landholding and public office.
1728	Franchise removed from Catholics.
1791	Foundation of United Irishmen republican movement.
1796	French invasion force lands in Bantry Bay.
1798	Defeat of Rising in Wexford and death of United Irishmen leaders Wolfe Tone and Lord Edward Fitzgerald.
1800	Act of Union between England and Ireland.
1803	Dublin Rising under Robert Emmet.
1829	Catholics allowed to sit in Parliament.
1845-1849	The Great Hunger: thousands starve to death as potato crop fails and thousands more emigrate.
1856	Phoenix Society founded.
1858	Irish Republican Brotherhood established.
1873	Foundation of Home Rule League.
1893	Foundation of Gaelic League.
1904	Foundation of Irish Reform Association.
1913	Dublin strikes and lockout.
1916	Easter Rising in Dublin and proclamation of an Irish Republic.
1917	Irish Parliament formed after Sinn Fein election victory.
1919-1921	War between Irish Republican Army and British Army.
1922	Irish Free State founded, while six northern counties remain part of United Kingdom as Northern Ireland, or Ulster; civil war up until 1923 between rival republican groups.
1949	Foundation of Irish Republic after all remaining constitutional links with Britain are severed.